BIO
PAYTON

33577000626901
Gallagher, Aileen.

Walter Payton

FOOTBALL HALL OF FAMERS

WALTER PAYTON

Aileen Gallagher

the rosen publishing group's
rosen
central

To The Dad, my favorite football fan

Published in 2003 by The Rosen Publishing Group, Inc.
29 East 21st Street, New York, NY 10010

First Edition

Library of Congress Cataloging-in-Publication Data

Gallagher, Aileen.
Walter Payton/Aileen Gallagher.— 1st ed.
p. cm. — (Football hall of famers)
Includes bibliographical references (p.) and index.
Summary: A biography of the record-setting Chicago Bears
fullback who died in 1999 at the age of forty-five.
ISBN 0-8239-3611-2 (lib. bdg.)
1. Payton, Walter, 1954–1999—Juvenile literature.
2. Football players—United States—Biography—Juvenile
literature. [1. Payton, Walter, 1954–1999. 2. Football
players. 3. African Americans—Biography.]
I. Title. II. Series.
GV939.P39 G35 2003
796.332'092—dc21

                                          2001007931

Manufactured in the United States of America

Contents

Introduction   5

1. Setting the Standard   12

2. A Quiet Excellence   23

3. Small Bear in a Big City   36

4. Sweetness Shines   50

5. Super Bowl Shuffle   65

6. Taking Care of Business   78

7. Sweetness Fading   88

Timeline   100

Glossary   102

For More Information   104

For Further Reading   106

Bibliography   107

Index   109

Walter Payton, known as "Sweetness," was one of the most successful running backs in NFL history.

Introduction

Walter Payton was probably not the best running back ever to play football, but he was one of the best talents to ever play the game. He holds the record for most career yards, at 16,726 yards on 3,838 carries. He scored 110 touchdowns in his career and helped the Chicago Bears defeat the New England Patriots in Super Bowl XX in 1985.

But those are just numbers.

Payton was known to football fans across the country as "Sweetness." No one, not even Payton, could say for sure where the nickname came from. For fans, the name described how he looked when he ran with a football—just plain sweet. For friends and others who knew him, "Sweetness" summed up his kind and giving personality. Either way, "Sweetness" defined Walter Payton, Number 34.

Payton was an all-around player. He could run, he could block, and he could pass. In college, at Jackson State University in Jackson, Mississippi, he was even used as a kicker. As a professional, he played quarterback during one game after all the other quarterbacks were injured. His talents led him not only to a Super Bowl but also to the Pro Football Hall of Fame, where the best of the best are honored.

Payton was a talented athlete from a young age. He began playing organized football only in his junior year of high school, after he traded his drums and marching band uniform for shoulder pads and cleats. Payton played for the first integrated high school team in his town's history, letting everyone know that black players were just as good as white players.

Though he was famous, Payton was a private person. His family—his wife, Connie; daughter, Brittney; and son, Jarrett—was more important to him than anything. When

Even at the height of his football career, Walter Payton, shown here with his wife, Connie, and his son, Jarrett, preferred to spend time with his family away from the public eye.

not playing football, Sweetness kept to himself. He did not like to give television or newspaper interviews and tried to avoid the media. Even during games, Payton wasn't much of a talker. He kept his mouth shut until the game was over and his job was done. Then, with his teammates and his family, he could be himself and joke around. From the early days when he and his brother, Eddie, played tricks on their sister, Pam, Payton was a prankster. When he was a professional, he would set off firecrackers during training camp. Years later, many of his former teammates could remember the days Payton played jokes on them.

There was a time and place for joking around, and the football field wasn't it. Sweetness took his job seriously, often by working harder and longer than most of the other players. In high school, he trained on his own to make sure he was the best, and his approach to the National Football League was no different. His parents, who worked hard all their lives, taught their children that nothing less than the best was acceptable.

In college, Payton's coach, Bob Hill, rein-
forced this message. Hill taught his players football fundamentals and every aspect of the game.
Payton learned a solid, simple approach to
football from Coach Hill that would help him
break the career rushing record in 1984. Where
other running backs tried to avoid tacklers by
running around them, Payton appeared to go
right through them. His aggressive style—
shoulders down, knees kicking high with every
step—took him to the record books and Canton, Ohio, home of the Hall of Fame.

Not just a football player, Payton was a
businessman who owned restaurants, a construction equipment business, and a race car
team. He came close to owning his own NFL
team, too. He donated his time and money to
help provide Christmas gifts to poor children in
Chicago and throughout Illinois.

All the energy Payton dedicated to his family, football, business, and charity came to a
halt in 1998, when Sweetness got sick. He had a
rare liver disease called primary sclerosing
cholangitis. While he was waiting for a liver

Eddie Payton *(right)* presents the Walter Payton Award to Louis Ivory on December 4, 2000. The award commemorates Payton's stellar achievements in Division I-AA.

transplant, his only chance of survival, Payton was diagnosed with bile duct cancer. This diagnosis meant that he could not get a transplant and that he would die. Sweetness passed away on November 1, 1999.

His name lives on in record books—most career rushing yards and youngest player (at age 23) to be named the NFL's most valuable player in 1977. He is immortalized in the Hall of Fame, and the Walter Payton Award is given every year to the best college football player from a Division I-AA team. As a player, Walter Payton's legacy has yet to be matched. His records still stand, and his talent is remembered by anyone who ever saw him play as pure "sweetness."

Setting the Standard

On the gridiron and off, Walter Payton was always on the move. He tore down the field clutching a football and then, after games, he would often dodge and weave his way past the sports reporters who wanted to write about him. He had been a mover since childhood.

Walter Payton was born on July 25, 1954, in Columbia, Mississippi. At the time of Payton's birth, Columbia had a population of about 7,500. The town's biggest employer was a parachute factory, where Payton's parents, Edward and Alyne, worked. When he wasn't working as a custodian at the factory, Payton's father did odd jobs for extra money. The Paytons weren't rich, but they had enough. No one else in the neighborhood had much either, so money was not a big issue to the Payton kids.

Walter Payton was the youngest of three children. He constantly played sports with his brother, Eddie, and sister, Pam. Playing was not only fun, but it was a way to get out of the house; if Alyne Payton ever caught her children with spare time on their hands, she would find something for them to do. Sometimes Walter hid in the outhouse, just so he wouldn't have to do chores.

Walter and Eddie often teamed up to play pranks on their sister. Sometimes Walter and Eddie rigged a bucket full of water over a door, soaking Pam when she opened it. Frequently, Pam would get scared at night and would crawl into her brothers' room. Once, they had rigged up a sheet on a string outside the window, terrifying their sister, who thought it was a ghost. "Did they ever do anything nice? I can't recall," Pam laughingly told reporter Don Pierson of the *Chicago Tribune.*

It was in the back lots and fields of Columbia that Walter Payton learned the lessons that would take him all the way to the Pro Football Hall of Fame. His father taught the Payton siblings that if you were going to play at all, you had to play your best. He was just as demanding of excellence off the playing field. Edward Payton had a garden outside the town, and he often took his three children there to help him cultivate the five-acre space. The work was tough, but Edward and Alyne Payton had no time for complaints. Later on, Walter found himself repeating his father's words, "Just do it right," to his own children.

All his life, people asked how Walter Payton got to be so strong. It all started with a hundred pounds of topsoil. Every summer, Alyne Payton would have a big load of topsoil delivered to the Payton house on Hendrick Street. It was Walter's and Eddie's job to spread the soil all over the yard. They did it one heavy wheelbarrow-load at a time, using the only shovel they had. Walter would fill the wheelbarrow, and Eddie would push it. It rains a lot in the summer in Mississippi, and Walter would always remember how the wheelbarrow sank into the soggy yard.

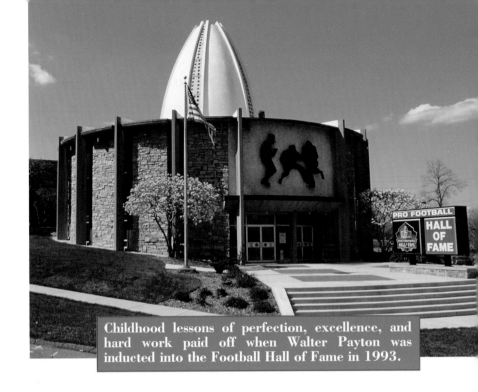

Childhood lessons of perfection, excellence, and hard work paid off when Walter Payton was inducted into the Football Hall of Fame in 1993.

It wasn't until years later that Payton realized his mother didn't need dirt spread all over the yard, but she did need to keep her boys out of trouble while school was out for the summer. Pam didn't have to push dirt around, but she was kept equally busy helping in the house and her mother's backyard garden. Payton got a lot out of pushing that dirt around. Besides gaining an understanding of hard work and a good set of muscles, the future record breaker learned to stick with something even when it seemed futile.

Payton's sense of style on the football field came from his youth. He used to play a game by himself called "war," where he would be both the good guy and the bad guy. When the neighborhood kids played tag, Payton would spin and jump and dance out of the way to keep from being "it." As he grew older, Payton took the techniques from his childhood games and applied them to the game of football. "When I held the football and somebody was going to take my football, I was going to hit them back first. I worked for that position and I wasn't giving it up or backing down," he said in his autobiography, *Never Die Easy*.

The pickup football games in the neighborhood taught Payton a lot, too. There were never enough kids for full teams, so they played from a hash mark to the sideline on the local high school's field. The field was so small that it forced Payton to learn the style that made him famous. The tiny field left little room for maneuvering, so Payton would jump over or run through the defense. When he later played on regulation-sized fields, Payton still resisted the urge to run around the defense or otherwise avoid them. He always faced them head-on.

Bridging Black and White

When Walter Payton was growing up, the schools in Columbia were segregated, which meant that black children and white children went to separate schools. The year he was born, 1954, the United States Supreme Court ruled that segregation was illegal in a landmark case called *Brown v. Board of Education.* But change was slow in coming to many parts of the South, including Columbia. There, Payton went to Jefferson High School while white kids went to the more modern Columbia High. It was not until 1970, halfway through Payton's junior year of high school, that the *Brown* decision was enforced and all of Columbia's children attended school together. At this time, Payton and his Jefferson classmates became students at Columbia High School.

Before going to Columbia, Payton had played football at Jefferson for only one season. During his first two years in high school, he played drums in the marching band. It was

WAITING ROOM
FOR WHITE ONLY
←
BY ORDER
POLICE DEPT.

Signs like this were commonplace during Payton's childhood in Mississippi, which like many other southern states, enforced racial segregation.

Eddie Payton, three years older than Walter, who was the star football player. Because Walter joined the team as a running back only after Eddie accepted a football scholarship to Jackson State University, people in Columbia thought Walter didn't want to compete with his brother on the field. Walter always denied this, saying that he played the drums until he figured out that girls liked boys in football uniforms better than band uniforms.

The football team played an important role in the integration of Columbia High School. Word around town was that the Jefferson team was better than the Columbia team. Columbia had better facilities and equipment, but Jefferson had more raw talent. No matter how many games Jefferson won, it was the Columbia players who were always in the newspaper and who always had better attendance at games. But with integration, the city had a chance to have a great football team.

As Payton and his teammates remembered, during the first season of integration, any tension on the field had more to do with each team trying to prove that it was the best rather than with racism. As he would do as a pro, Payton let his talents and personality shine. The white students from Columbia had never seen such a good running back. And Payton's playful personality—made known by his practical jokes at others' expense—made him well liked by everyone on the team, black and white.

Payton also showed his team that he took football seriously by being in better shape than almost anyone on the Columbia team. Payton never said much about exercise, but his teammates knew all about his personal training program. He jogged to and from practice every day from his home, which was over a mile from school. And when Payton wasn't running to practice, he would put on a pair of old army boots that he had found at the city dump and run through the woods, darting around trees as though they were defensive linemen. After clunking around in army boots, football cleats felt like slippers.

It was in a game against Prentiss High School that Payton made the most memorable play of his high school career. The game occurred in 1970, Payton's senior year. The Columbia Wildcats were down 6–0 in the first half when Payton got the ball and ran it 95 yards, straight into the end zone. He scored again from 65 yards out later in the game, helping the Wildcats win 14–6. The game was a victory for both Payton and the newly integrated Columbia High. It was the first game after integration, and the victory helped people in town see the team as just that—a team of kids playing a game—instead of black and white players battling it out on a field. Columbia hadn't won a lot before integration, but the Wildcats took seven straight games that first year. The team and the town were so excited about winning that they didn't think about much else, according to Payton's coach, Charles Boston.

An All-Around Athlete

Walter Payton attributed much of his later football and business success to playing sports at Columbia High. Besides football, he played baseball and basketball, and went out for track, where he was a sprinter. At one track meet, Coach Boston (who coached all of Payton's teams at Columbia) asked Payton to fill in for an injured long jumper. Payton had never competed in the long jump before and didn't even know how to do it. But Coach Boston gave him a quick lesson, and Payton took a few practice jumps. That was all he needed. In one jump, Payton not only won the event and helped his team win the meet, but he also set the track meet record and became the state champion long jumper. As he recalled in his autobiography, *Never Die Easy*, "That was just one of many days where life in Columbia gave me the confidence to do bigger things later on."

A Quiet Excellence

If Walter Payton had graduated from high school in 1991 instead of 1971, he likely would have been recruited by some of the country's best college football programs. But in 1971, the big football powerhouses—especially in the South—were recruiting few black athletes. Players who wanted to go to the large schools with well-known programs and excellent facilities had to go far from home. Since most of these kids came from small towns or rural areas, leaving home was a difficult choice.

The Southeastern Conference (SEC), made up of such schools as Texas A&M, Mississippi State, and the University of Kentucky, chose to ignore the deep talent pool in its own backyard. At that time, only white students played for this premier southern college league. It was not until

In 1974, Payton was at the height of his success at Jackson State College, having become college football's all-time scoring champion.

1967 that a black player even took the field at an SEC school. Four years later, when Payton went to college, little had changed. The SEC schools all had a few black players, but the schools snubbed most of the young talent.

Jackson State Comes Calling

For the rest of his career, Coach Boston would remember the day some scouts from the University of Southern Mississippi came to look at Columbia receiver Steve Stewart, who was white. Boston asked the scouts repeatedly why they didn't go for Payton. "We just want Steve," Boston remembered the scouts saying. "Imagine a program like Southern Mississippi not wanting a player like Walter Payton, who makes all-state and becomes the NFL's all-time leading rusher and he grows up thirty miles away," Boston said in *Never Die Easy*.

Even though Payton was named all-state his senior year of high school, only three schools offered him a football scholarship: the University of Kansas, Alcorn State, and Jackson State. Payton was one of the best high

Jackson State University officials announce plans to build the Walter Payton Athletic Complex, a 22-acre sports facility in honor of its former star player.

school players in the country, but because he was black, Payton was offered a chance to play for only one nationally ranked team, the University of Kansas. Alcorn and Jackson were both Mississippi state schools, with traditionally black-only student bodies. They were also part of the National Collegiate Athletic Association's Division I-AA, a group of smaller schools that doesn't get as much funding or attention as Division I-A schools like Penn State or the University of Alabama. Kansas was a big school, but it was too far from home for Payton. Both

Alcorn and Jackson would become part of an athletic league called the Southwestern Athletic Conference (SWAC), which was organized in 1974, Payton's final year of college.

Though Payton's beloved Coach Boston was a graduate of Alcorn, Payton chose Jackson State. His brother, Eddie, was already attending the school on scholarship, and many other Columbia teammates were also playing there. Walter's freshman year was the last time he and his brother would play football together. They were both backs, and fans named their part of the field "Paytons' Place." Looking back, Payton said Jackson State was a great place for him because it was small enough to keep him grounded. Football players at Jackson State were not the celebrities they would have been at the larger programs. The team didn't have the fancy facilities or equipment that could be found at SEC schools.

Being part of a great team in a college that was virtually ignored by the press may have stung Payton at the time, but he later said it did him a lot of good. Players at the big schools were

The Payton brothers, Walter *(left)* and Eddie, faced each other in this 1982 NFL game. Eddie's Minnesota Vikings won 35–7.

spoiled, he thought. With newspapers and television saying all the time how great the teams were, the players started to believe it. The coaches at the big schools made a lot of money and the teams' football boosters, groups of fans that raised money for the teams, contributed even more to the programs. All that added up to two things in Payton's opinion: big egos and terrible pressure to perform.

The Coach Who Set the Standard

The man who would keep Payton grounded at Jackson State was his coach, Bob Hill. "He kept it real," Payton said about the coach in *Never Die Easy*. Hill was known for his coaching throughout the state. Like Payton, Hill took the game of football seriously. He had no interest in end-zone dances or players who drew attention to themselves. Hill said that they were a joke. Anyone on his Jackson State Tigers team would find himself riding the bench if he pulled any antics on the field. Payton shared this opinion and took it with him into the pros, earning the respect of players across the National Football League in the process.

Hill's strict emphasis on the basics of football helped make Payton a complete player, one who was good at every aspect of the game. He could run the ball fast and hard. He could catch a football with one hand. During practice, Hill regularly had Payton block guys who were bigger than he was. Payton's blocking prowess became his calling card in the NFL. Hill also had his players learn to do a bit of everything. While he played for the Tigers, Payton was a kicker, taking care of extra points and field goals.

At Jackson State, Payton began what would become a habit in his professional career: He never missed a game. Once, when his ankle hurt, Payton asked the trainers to tape it tight enough so that he could play. First, the trainers taped the skin. Then, Payton put on his sock and had it taped again. Finally, he put on his shoe and the ankle was taped yet again. "I gained one hundred something yards and scored a couple of touchdowns that day," he recalled in *Never Die Easy*.

Like every great coach, Hill was loved by his players, but they also feared and respected him at the same time. That fear made his team keep their act together—if anyone caused a problem, he would have to answer to Coach Hill. The coach kept a special eye on Payton; their relationship was more father-son than it was coach-player. It was Hill who introduced Payton to Connie Norwood, who would one day become the player's wife.

Dancing into Her Heart

The first time Connie Norwood saw Walter Payton, he was on television. Payton's footwork was just as good on the dance floor as it was on the football field. He and a dance partner won a competition on a local Jackson television show. The prize was a trip to Los Angeles to appear on the famous dance program *Soul Train*. Though she didn't know it then, Connie's future husband was there on *Soul Train*, with bell bottoms and platform shoes. Connie met Walter in person when she was a senior in high school. Bob Hill was dating Connie's aunt, and the coach thought Connie was levelheaded and wouldn't be starstruck by Walter's football skills. He knew Connie would love Walter for Walter, not because he was a football star. When Connie decided to go to college at Jackson State, she and Walter became an item. They would be together for the rest of Walter's life.

Walter had found in Connie the only thing that mattered to him more than football. But of course, there was still football. Together with his teammates, Payton and the Jackson State

Never Die Easy

As a running back, Payton would constantly have to dodge linebackers. Many running backs avoid this part of the job by running out of bounds when they're about to get hit. But Payton would run right into the opposing team. Doing so would let linebackers know he was there and that he wasn't afraid of them, Payton said. Coach Hill had a motto for this style of play: Never die easy. Payton adopted the motto as his own, and it eventually became the title of his autobiography. To never die easy means to never give up without a fight. As a running back, never dying easy means never running out of bounds unless you hit someone on your way out.

Walter Payton *(left)* won the Black College All-American Offensive Player of the Year Award in 1974 while playing for Jackson State.

Tigers would dominate the SWAC. Twenty of the Tigers who shared the field with Payton in his four years at Jackson State would eventually be drafted by the NFL. Other SWAC schools, such as Grambling, in Georgia, and Alcorn, in Mississippi, boasted similar talent.

While Payton played football for the Jackson State Tigers, he was the best in the league. Had the media been paying attention, Payton likely would have been recognized as the best college football player in the country. From 1971 to 1975, the Tigers' record was 33-11-1. Payton rushed for 3,563 career yards, averaging 6.1 yards per carry. He scored 66 touchdowns in college, a national record. Just as in high school, the press paid attention to the schools that fronted white teams. Payton was constantly passed over for awards—awards that went to players who weren't necessarily as good as he was, but who were white.

Payton graduated from Jackson State in 1974. He completed his course work early and got a bachelor of science in education in three and a half years, six months sooner than most students. Payton was ready to prove himself as a professional football player. In the NFL, Payton would not run into the sort of racial barriers he did as a college player. While color lines still existed in the NFL, Payton was often a leader in moving those lines. Never again would he be overlooked by the media simply because he was black. Instead, they would look at him not as a black player or a white one, but as a Bear—a Chicago Bear.

Small Bear in a Big City

3

The Chicago Bears drafted Walter Payton in 1975. Soon after, he realized that he wasn't just going to play for a football team—he was going to play for the entire city of Chicago. Chicago, then and now, is a hardworking city. Payton was one of the hardest-working football players in the game, and the people of Chicago recognized and loved him for it. He was also one of the biggest celebrities in Chicago. Though other famous athletes came before and after him, the relationship Payton had with his adopted city was unique. Other athletes knew it, including Michael Jordan, the spectacular basketball player who played for the Chicago Bulls: "Walter was a Chicago icon long before I arrived there," Jordan said in a statement released shortly after Payton's death.

The Chicago skyline. Chicago was daunting and unfamiliar for Payton, but he soon made it his home, becoming a city hero in the process.

Chicago's harsh weather perfectly suited Payton's game. In the Windy City, catching a football in November is one of the most difficult tasks in sports. It's fitting that Chicago's football franchise would work the field by running the ball as a team and not by highlighting the abilities of a few with some fancy passes. Payton was made for a team that depended on its running backs and linemen.

A Hope for the Future

At the time of the 1975 draft, Chicago was looking for a new running back. The "best" in the country was Archie Griffin, an Ohio State player who had won the Heisman Trophy twice. The Chicago Bears liked to think of themselves as a team that took chances, and they approached the draft that way as well. Previous first-round draft picks had come from smaller schools, and those players had done well. Payton, who racked up impressive numbers in college and was twice named a Little All-American, was not a tremendous draft risk. For Chicago, which was more of a workhorse team than a winning team, Payton was an excellent prospect.

Payton was the Bears' first choice in the draft, but another team also had its eye on the 20-year-old running back from Jackson State. The Dallas Cowboys had the second pick that year, and the coaching staff was arguing over how that pick would be used. Defensive coaches wanted an offensive lineman named Randy White. The offensive coaches wanted Payton. Tom Landry, the Cowboys' head coach, sided with the defense. Chicago had the fourth pick and snapped up Payton immediately.

The Chicago Bears chose Walter Payton over Heisman Trophy winner Archie Griffin, shown here, even though Griffin was considered the best running back that season.

On draft day, Payton glowed with confidence. He knew that Chicago had a history of great backs, the players who block the defense and run with the ball. The most recent was Gayle Sayers, who played for the Bears between 1965 and 1971. Payton invoked this legendary name at a press conference with the Bears. "If the people of Chicago give me some time and are patient, I'll give them a new Gayle Sayers," he predicted. Someone must have believed him because Payton signed a three-year contract that day, worth $450,000.

As usual, Payton appeared unshakable to the outside world. He seemed completely sure of himself. But on the inside, the young player was nervous. Chicago was cold. And it was in the North, a place Payton hadn't spent a lot of time in. One of the biggest cities he had ever been to was Jackson, Mississippi, which was nothing much compared to the famed Windy City. As he often did when he had problems, Payton talked to his mother. In *Never Die Easy*, he recalled what she told him: "This is what has been dealt and you need to play your hand out."

Despite his apprehension, Payton knew he had a job to do. In his neighborhood, the guys who were lucky enough to go to college usually became teachers or preachers, respected positions in black southern culture. Payton had an opportunity that so few people had, and he knew he couldn't mess it up. Playing football was a way to go to college and get a degree, but for a rare few, playing college football was a way

Payton's number, 34, was retired after his
12-year stint with the Chicago Bears.

to get to the NFL. Payton's anxiety was hitting
its peak right about the time he went to Bears
training camp for the first time. On the drive up
from Columbia, he went to visit his brother,
Eddie, then a teacher and coach in Memphis,

Tennessee. (Eddie Payton would also play in the NFL, but he would not join the Detroit Lions until 1977.) Eddie offered his younger brother a piece of advice that helped carry him through those first difficult weeks. Walter recounted his brother's words in *Never Die Easy*: "Walter, just don't fumble. The only way they'll cut you is if you fumble. So don't."

He didn't fumble, and he played with fervor from day one. Payton's new teammates had never seen anything like him. Linebacker Doug Buffone remembered the first practice in *College and Pro Football Newsweekly*: "Walter gets the ball and comes right at me and runs me over. He does the same thing the very next play. I wasn't going to let it happen the next time. He comes at me and I hit him as hard as I can. He pops up and the next snap, here he comes again. He was relentless from the very beginning."

He might not have fumbled, but Payton's first game with the Bears was nothing special. The ball was in his possession eight times, but he failed to gain a single yard. The Bears lost

35–7 to the Baltimore Colts. After the game, Payton wept. The rest of his rookie season, 1975–1976, wasn't much better. The Bears had a losing record of 4-10. Payton carried the ball only 679 yards the entire season. On average, he moved only 3.5 yards per carry. He scored 7 touchdowns. Throughout the rest of his career as a pro, the statistics from that first game would echo in Payton's head. "Zero yards," he would repeat over and over during the years of training that followed. "Zero yards."

His first season was notable for one other statistic: Payton missed a game, this one against the Pittsburgh Steelers. Coach Jack Pardee was concerned about Payton's ankle, which was sore. The running back assured his coach he could play, but Pardee wanted to be safe and sat Payton out. It was the only game in his 13 seasons as a pro that Payton missed. Since he was willing and ready to play, Payton never counted it as a game "missed due to injury," as the statistics indicate. Playing in every game was a source of pride to Payton and a very important statistic to him personally.

Payton makes a trademark leap over a fallen teammate, going on to make a 24-yard return on a kickoff during his first season with Chicago.

Another event of that first season began a habit that would last through his entire career. On his first away game as a Bear, Payton sat in the first window seat on the left side of the coach section of the plane. Though his rise in team stature would later allow Payton to move up to first class, Payton always sat in coach. For every single away game of his career, he sat in that same seat on the plane. His teammates loved Payton for this small gesture that said, "I am one of you." Being part of a team was more important to Sweetness than being a star.

In his second season, feeling more comfortable in Chicago with Connie at his side, Payton began to get some of his moves back. He began to play the talented game that took him to the NFL in the first place. He rushed for 1,390 yards and scored 13 touchdowns. For the first time as a pro, he had the potential to make the record books, trailing only slightly behind the

Starting a Family

Payton's loneliness was tough on him during his first year with the Bears. For a man who had always been both physically and emotionally close to his family, being so far away from home was difficult. Connie was still at Jackson State. She would come to visit sometimes, but it wasn't enough for Payton—so they got married on July 7, 1976. The following day, Payton returned to Chicago to begin training for his second season as a Bear. The wedding was simple because it was rushed, but also because Connie didn't like parties.

Payton, unlike other running backs, didn't dodge the defensive line. Very often, as in this 1982 game against the New England Patriots, he simply jumped over them.

league's leading rusher, legend O.J. Simpson of the San Francisco 49ers. By Payton's third season in 1977, that rushing statistic grew to 1,852 yards and 14 touchdowns. The achievement earned him the title of the NFL's Most Valuable Player of the season. At 23, Payton was the youngest player to receive that honor.

As his yardage grew, so did his popularity in Chicago. Payton worked hard at being a good player, and the Chicago fans rewarded him with their unyielding enthusiasm. Fans elsewhere were wild about Payton, too: In the 1981 Thanksgiving Day game against the Dallas Cowboys, Payton's team lost 10–9, but the running back had moved the ball 179 yards on 38 carries. As he walked off the field after the last whistle, the Dallas crowd rose to their feet in appreciation of a true talent. Payton was also the first and only Chicago Bear to receive regular standing ovations at Lambeau Field, home of the Bears' hated rival, the Green Bay Packers.

With every season, Payton got better, his statistics improved, and his salary grew; by 1980, he was the highest-paid player in the league, making $450,000 a year. The average salary for an NFL player in 1980 was $117,000. He increased his rushing yards each season. In a 1977 game against the Minnesota Vikings, Payton ran the ball up and down the field almost three times, rushing 275 yards. Despite the effort, his team scored only 10 points and lost the game. The struggling Bears made football a challenge for Payton. He often thought of leaving the game, but he was unwilling to do so without at least having the opportunity to play in a play-off game. A Super Bowl would have been nice, too, but seemed an impossibly distant goal. With the team led by Coach Mike Ditka, a former Chicago Bear who became coach in 1982, Payton would get his chance.

Sweetness Shines

As a Bear, Payton wore number 34. With a trademark white sweatband on his head and the nickname Sweetness, Payton was on his way to being a Chicago icon even before he broke the all-time rushing record or helped the Bears win a Super Bowl. During all the years the Bears lost games, the team never lost heart, and Walter Payton had a hand in this. He became an even bigger practical joker than when he was a young boy trying to scare his sister. One of Payton's favorite standbys was firecrackers—big ones. The giant M-80s would explode in the middle of the night during pre-season, waking the exhausted players who were trying to sleep off the pain from twice-a-day practices. Payton was always responsible for the explosions.

The white headband was so much a part of Walter Payton's football persona that it appears in many of the running back's official team photos. Some people considered his Bears uniform incomplete without it.

For all his fun and jokes, Payton grew increasingly dedicated to his team and his game as the years wore on. When Coach Mike Ditka arrived in Chicago from the Dallas Cowboys in 1982, all the elements were in place for Payton to become one of the all-time greats. Ditka recognized and loved Payton for his strong work ethic. Ditka knew that Payton believed the team was good enough to get to the Super Bowl and win.

However, to achieve such a goal would take a lot of teamwork. In the early 1980s, Payton's best friend on the team, fullback Roland Harper, was struggling with injured knees. Harper and Payton shared similar backgrounds—both came from the South and had attended small, black colleges. Their relationship was teamwork at its best—Harper protected Payton, blocking opposing players so that Payton could run the ball. Harper retired from football, and Payton trucked on without him. Payton knew that he would have to retire someday, too, and watching Harper was like a glimpse into the future. But what Payton didn't expect was that Harper's replacement, Matt

The Bears' coach Mike Ditka was instrumental in honing Payton's talent and helping him become one of football's best running backs.

Suhey, would become not only a trusted teammate but also a close friend.

Best Friends

Suhey and Payton were an unlikely duo; they were as different as Harper and Payton were similar. Suhey was white and had been the third generation in his family to play for Penn State, one of the biggest and best football schools in the country. Suhey's family was educated, whereas Payton's parents were not. Payton, though open and friendly with his teammates, avoided the press, but Suhey enjoyed talking to reporters. Like Harper, Suhey learned to anticipate Payton's moves on the field and make the blocks Payton needed to carry the ball.

In one of Suhey's earliest memories of Payton, recounted in *Never Die Easy*, Suhey had fumbled going in for a touchdown and was very angry at himself for messing up. As he and Payton were leaving the field, Payton asked Suhey if he had ever had a paper route. Suhey had no idea what Payton was talking about, and said so. Payton looked at his friend, smirked, and said, "Do that again and you better find yourself a paper route, because you sure won't be playing no more football."

With the Chicago Bears, whether it was in the locker room or on the line, there was no distinction between black and white. The respect and trust everyone on the team had for each other helped the team function as a strong unit.

Running for the Record

For running backs, the record to beat belonged to Jim Brown, who rushed for 12,312 career

The Practical Joker

Sweetness had a high-pitched voice, which could easily be disguised to sound like a woman's. Payton liked nothing better than calling his teammates' wives and pretending to be a girlfriend. The wives would be furious, and the players had a hard time convincing them the "woman" was just Payton. He also loved to go to the Bears' office between practices and use the same voice to answer the phone there. He enjoyed causing confusion.

Another favorite Payton prank was one he pulled on Bears safety Dave Duerson, who was playing in his first NFC Pro Bowl Squad a few days after the Bears won Super Bowl XX in 1985. Duerson was excited to be in beautiful, breezy Hawaii with the best players in the NFC. "After about three minutes it started getting awfully warm," Duerson told Larry Mayer of the *Chicago Bear Report*. "Walter had put some unscented liquid heat in my jock [strap]. It was a very hot afternoon in warm, sunny Hawaii."

yards during nine seasons with the Cleveland Browns. Brown was a star in college, where he played for the Syracuse University Orangemen. But besides his higher-profile football background, Brown was similar to Payton. Both were workhorses with similar running styles. Like Payton, Brown was an attacker who considered it weak to run out-of-bounds to protect himself from tackles. Payton had no fear of tackles. Dan Pompei, a columnist for *The Sporting News*, estimated that Sweetness was hit at least 7,000 times in his professional career.

At the beginning of the 1984 season, Payton had rushed for 11,625 career yards. Another player, Franco Harris, had 11,950 career yards, mostly with the Pittsburgh Steelers. Harris had recently signed with the Seattle Seahawks. Both men wanted to beat Brown's record. Everyone in football knew it would happen that season. The question was simply who would do it first.

Brown was proud of his record and wanted to keep it, if he could. In the summer of 1984, at age 47, the long-retired player threatened to

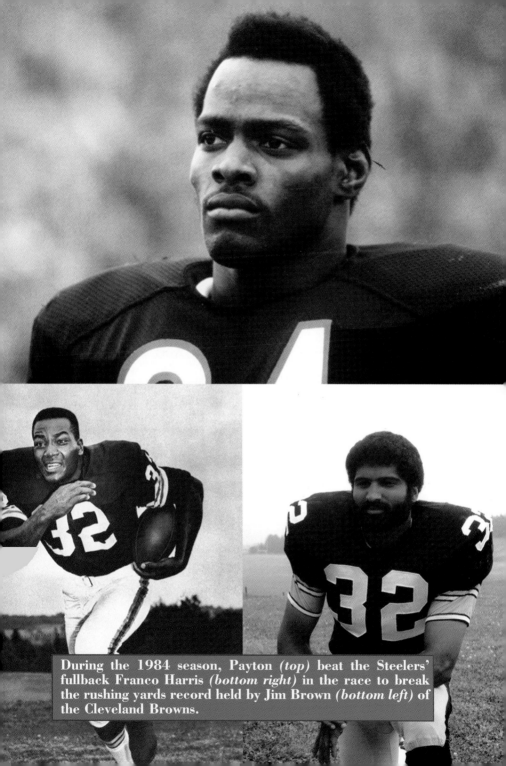

During the 1984 season, Payton *(top)* beat the Steelers' fullback Franco Harris *(bottom right)* in the race to break the rushing yards record held by Jim Brown *(bottom left)* of the Cleveland Browns.

start playing again to make sure he remained the man who carried the ball for more yards than anyone else. Harris was a player who often ran out-of-bounds, and Brown publicly criticized him for doing so.

Payton never doubted Harris's abilities. After all, he was the man who had helped the Steelers win four Super Bowls. Off the field, the Payton and Harris families were friends, and Payton had had some business dealings with Harris. The press constantly asked Payton how he felt about Harris's running style. Though he chose not to run out-of-bounds, that didn't mean anyone else couldn't, Sweetness told reporters. Payton was not going to allow the media to drag him into a personal confrontation with Harris, he wrote in *Never Die Easy*. The two of them chasing the record was competition enough.

Payton's biggest leap ahead of Harris came during a game against the Seahawks. In the game, Payton rushed for 116 yards while Harris got only 23. All the Bears' linemen were supporting Payton that entire season, taking the hits that would help their man win the record. He did it on October 7, 1984, at a home game at Chicago's Soldier Field against the New Orleans Saints.

Payton entered the game only 66 yards short of Brown's record. He broke the record simply and methodically. The play that surpassed Brown was a simple one—a six-yard run during the second carry of the second half. The minute Payton won the record, the Bears wanted to stop the game and hold a short ceremony, but Payton requested that the team not make a huge deal out of it. In the end, they stopped the game momentarily and there was an announcement over the stadium's public address system. On the field, the Bears congratulated Payton, and then he went to the sidelines and shook hands with the Saints' coach, Bum Phillips. Finally, he tossed the game ball to Johnny Roland, the Bears' running back coach.

Privately, Payton had mixed emotions. Breaking the record was proof that he had worked hard and performed well over several seasons, not just during one play or one game.

Walter Payton leaps over the line to score a touchdown against the New Orleans Saints in the 1984 game in which he broke the record for career rushing yards.

The record was proof of his consistency. It had been a goal for him to work toward, but after he broke it, Payton still felt funny about it. To him, Brown still held the record because it had taken Payton more seasons to rush that many yards. As Payton said in his autobiography, "I didn't do it in the amount of time that Jim Brown did. I had more games and I played longer. So I didn't break it."

As far as fans, the press, and his teammates were concerned, the record now belonged to Payton. He set a new standard for all other running backs. By the time he retired in 1987, Payton had rushed for 16,726 yards. "I want to set the record so high that the next person who tries for it, it's going to bust his heart," Payton told the Associated Press.

One glory continued to elude Payton: He still didn't have a Super Bowl ring. In his record-breaking season of 1984, the Bears had their first shot at making it to the NFL championship. In the first round of the play-offs, the Bears traveled to Washington, D.C., to play the

Redskins on December 30. The Redskins were the defending NFC champions. The Chicago Bears hadn't won a play-off game since 1963, and no one thought that game would be anything other than a loss. But Payton knew better. He led the Bears' attack, throwing the ball in a pass play that ended in a touchdown and rushing for more than 100 yards. The Bears took the game, 23–19. The team then tried to carry the momentum to the NFC championship game against the San Francisco 49ers. Their heart and hard work couldn't beat the legendary quarterback Joe Montana and his Niners.

When the Bears lost the NFC championship to San Francisco, Payton was heartbroken. The team lost 23–0—an embarrassing shutout. Jim McMahon was out of the game with a lacerated kidney. Backup quarterback Steve Fuller completed only 13 of 22 passes and got only 87 passing yards. Payton rushed for 92 yards that game, on 22 carries. But that wasn't enough for Payton. "Next time, bring your offense," teased the 49ers' safety Ronnie Lott as Payton walked off the field, according to Bob LeGere in *Pro Football Weekly*. The next opportunity would be the 1985 season. In that season, Chicago would bring everything it had to every game. San Francisco would go on to beat the Miami Dolphins 28–16 in Super Bowl XIX. In 1985, the Bears vowed, they would win a championship for the city of Chicago.

5 Super Bowl Shuffle

The loss to the 49ers was difficult for Walter Payton. It had taken him 10 years with the Bears to get that close, and he feared it would take another 10 to get a second chance. Payton knew his body wouldn't last that long, so he made sure that the 1985 Chicago Bears were the best team anyone had ever seen.

Running for the Super Bowl

Between Ditka and Payton, the team was mentally primed to rule the NFL in the 1985 season. Mike Singletary, the Bears' middle linebacker that year, said in *Never Die Easy* that the whole team noticed a new intensity of focus in Payton. Payton, never a talkative player during games, suddenly began to speak up in huddles. Payton's teammates were encouraged by his belief that

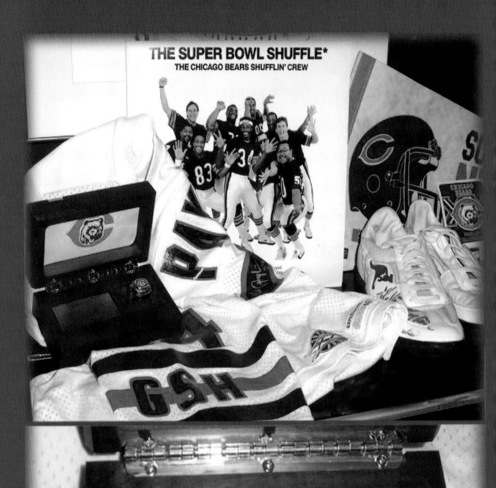

This montage of Walter Payton memorabilia includes Payton's jersey, cleats, and Super Bowl Ring; the Bears' Super Bowl Banner; and the jacket from the 1985 Bears' record single "The Super Bowl Shuffle."

they could go all the way to Super Bowl XX. In the 1985 season, their enthusiasm showed in victory after victory.

The team's enthusiasm was so great that they recorded a song, with an accompanying video, called "The Super Bowl Shuffle," which sold more than a million copies. As a whole, the team played better than it had since Payton joined the struggling Bears in 1975. The team won its first 12 games and looked forward to a perfect season.

The only flaw was their loss to the Miami Dolphins, which in 1972 was the last NFL team to go undefeated. Although Payton rushed for 121 yards in that game, the Bears lost 38–24.

Despite the disappointment, the Bears refused to lose their momentum. In the postseason, Chicago steamrolled the Giants 21–0 and the Rams 24–0. There was only one game left to win: Super Bowl XX. At the New Orleans Superdome against the New England Patriots, Payton rushed for only 66 yards on 22 attempts. For him, these numbers were low. New England did everything possible to keep Payton off his feet. At times, it seemed like the entire Patriots' defensive line was determined to sweep Sweetness. Quarterback Jim McMahon remembers the Patriots' play this way in *Never Die Easy*: "Their downfall was worrying so much about Walter; they let everybody else have a pretty good day."

The Bears won the game 46–10, which, at that point, was the biggest Super Bowl win ever. To Payton, however, the game was initially a huge disappointment: Even though the team had scored a lot of touchdowns, Payton had failed to score even one—he just never got the ball. His coach, Mike Ditka, remembered it as one of the most disappointing realizations in Payton's career. Though he was upset, Payton wouldn't have wanted a staged touchdown just for his sake. In the end, he decided that for that particular game on that particular day, he just wasn't meant to score. After all, winning was what mattered most, and the people of Chicago—who had given so much to Payton and the Bears—were overjoyed by the victory.

At the beginning of the 1986 season, it seemed as though the Bears could do it all over again. The team won seven of its first eight games

Payton's head-on aggressive style helped the Chicago Bears win their only Super Bowl in 1986.

and finished the season with 14 wins and only 2 losses. But it was not to be. Payton thought that the dizzying thrill of the Super Bowl victory made it hard for many of his teammates to regain the focus that had taken them to New Orleans. Suddenly, everyone was famous, being written up in newspapers and magazines, doing commercials and public appearances. The players were so thrilled about winning Super Bowl XX that they could not concentrate on winning Super Bowl XXI. "It takes everybody to win a Super Bowl," Payton said in his autobiography. The Bears would not repeat their victory in 1986. With a record of 14-3, the team made it to the second round of the play-offs but lost to the underdog Washington Redskins, 27–13. The Bears were out of the postseason.

A Career Winds Down

Things were starting to change for Payton in 1987. He signed a one-year, $1 million contract, his last with the Bears. The Bears drafted Neal Anderson, a running back from the University of Florida. With Anderson on the field, it was clear to Payton that he was being phased out. His offensive stats for the season were the lowest of his career: He gained 533 yards on 146 carries. The Bears retired his number, 34, at halftime of his last regular season game. The Bears' publicist, Bill McGrane, noted in *Never Die Easy* that two fans held a sign that said, "Santa: Please send more Walter Paytons. First one was perfect." At the end of the game, which the Bears lost, Payton threw two balls into the stands. The gesture was a way of saying thank you to the people of Chicago, who had stood by the Bears for so many years.

Long after the game ended, Payton sat on the bench, in full uniform, looking out at Soldier Field. He wanted to remember what it felt like to look at the field as a player. He thought back on all of the great plays and hard-fought wins from his past. He wanted to hold on to how it felt to be Walter Payton, Chicago Bear. The next morning, he would just be Walter Payton, Regular Guy.

But he wasn't just a regular guy. With his career record—16,726 career rushing yards, 3,838 carries, and 110 touchdowns—Payton was insured a place in the Hall of Fame. He had

Payton after his last game. When he retired in 1988, Payton held the record for most rushing yards and had twice been named NFL Player of the Year.

won the NFC rushing title every year from 1976 to 1980. He had played in nine Pro Bowl games. He was named NFL Player of the Year in 1977 and 1985. When it came time for Hall of Fame officials to vote on the 1993 inductees, Payton was chosen in his first year of eligibility.

An induction speech is given for every player who enters the Hall of Fame in Canton, Ohio. Payton asked Jim Finks to give his speech. Finks was the general manager of the Bears, the man who had taken a chance and drafted the kid from Jackson State. At the time of the induction, Finks was dying from cancer and was unable to make the journey. Payton's next choice was his own son, Jarrett, then 12 years old. Jarrett Payton was the first child to introduce a parent at a Hall of Fame induction ceremony. Payton had no idea what his son would say until he made the speech.

On July 31, 1993, Jarrett's speech was short but meaningful. In part, he said, "Not only is my dad an exceptional athlete, he's a role model. He's my biggest role model and best friend. We do a lot of things together, play basketball, golf, go to the movies, to name a few. I'm sure my sister will endorse this statement: We have a super dad."

After Jarrett Payton said his piece, nearly everyone in the room was crying, including his father. Through his tears, Sweetness spoke to his children and his fans. "Everybody that you meet, you can learn something from them. Everybody that comes in your life can influence your life as well. Just as these people here have, just as you have, because the fans are what make this game. Without you being out here and coming to this Hall of Fame, it wouldn't be professional football. So I stand here and I applaud you for supporting

Payton hugs his son, Jarrett, after the 12-year-old made an introduction speech at Payton's 1993 induction ceremony into the Football Hall of Fame.

and staying with the National Football League and these players here. Thank you." Surrounded by family and friends while being recognized for his achievements, Payton missed only one thing during his Hall of Fame induction: his father.

Edward Payton had died in 1979, somewhat mysteriously. The elder Payton was driving around Columbia one night when he was pulled over by a white police officer and arrested for drunk driving. Since Edward Payton rarely drank, the family refused to believe that the charges were true. That same night, he died of a brain aneurysm in a jail cell. The family later figured he had already been suffering from the aneurysm when he was pulled over, making him off balance and difficult to understand, which made him appear drunk. The Payton family, raised as they were, eventually decided that whatever had happened couldn't be undone. But to Edward Payton's son, Walter, to whom family was the most important thing in the world, his father's presence on induction day was sorely missed.

Walter Payton's NFL Career Statistics

Regular Season

Rushing

Year	Att.	Yds.	Avg.	TD
1975	196	679	3.5	7
1976	311	1,390	4.5	13
1977	339	1,852	5.5	14
1978	333	1,395	4.2	11
1979	369	1,610	4.4	14
1980	317	1,460	4.6	6
1981	339	1,222	3.6	6
1982	148	596	4.0	1
1983	314	1,421	4.5	6
1984	381	1,684	4.4	11
1985	324	1,551	4.8	9
1986	321	1,333	4.2	8
1987	146	533	3.7	4
Total	3,838	16,726	4.4	110

Receiving

Year	Rec.	Yds.	Avg.	TD	G/GS
1975	33	213	6.5	0	13/7
1976	15	149	9.9	0	14/14
1977	27	269	10.0	2	14/14
1978	50	480	9.6	0	16/16
1979	31	313	10.1	2	16/16
1980	46	367	8.0	1	16/16
1981	41	379	9.2	2	16/16
1982	32	311	9.7	0	9/9
1983	53	607	11.5	2	16/16
1984	45	368	8.2	0	16/16
1985	49	483	9.9	2	16/16
1986	37	382	10.3	3	16/16
1987	33	217	6.6	1	12/12
Total	492	4,538	9.2	15	190/184

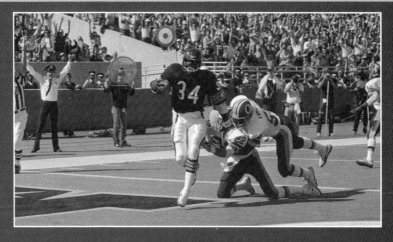

Play-Offs

Rushing

Year	No.	Yds.	Avg.	LG	TD
1977	19	60	3.1	11	0
1979	16	67	4.2	12	2
1984	46	196	4.3	20	0
1985	67	186	2.8	12	0
1986	14	38	2.7	9	0
1987	18	85	4.7	16	0
Total	180	632	3.5	20	2

Receiving

Year	No.	Yds.	Avg.	LG	TD	G/GS
1977	3	33	11.0	20	0	1/1
1979	3	52	17.3	31	0	1/1
1984	4	23	5.8	12	0	2/2
1985	8	52	6.5	19	0	3/3
1986	1	-2	-2.0	-2	0	1/1
1987	3	20	6.7	9	0	1/1
Total	22	178	8.3	31	0	9/9

Career Passing: 11-34-331, 8 TDs, 5 Interceptions

Career Kickoff Returns: 17 for 539 yards

Career Punting: 1 for 39 yards

Taking Care of Business

6

Retirement was a difficult choice for Payton. He was beginning to physically lose his edge, and he sensed the Bears' management wanting to go in different directions. The Bears had drafted a new running back for the 1987 season, and Payton believed he was being shown the door. His agent, Bud Holmes, had also raised the possibility of Payton owning a football team. Still, Sweetness had never done anything else in his life but play football. Summer had always meant training camp, fall was football season, and winter and spring were all about conditioning and preparing for the next season. In retirement, Payton would have to call his own plays. He was nervous and unsure, but he thought retirement would lead him to his next goal, owning a professional football team.

By 1993, Payton had various successful business ventures, though his dream of owning a football team remained unfulfilled.

After retiring, Payton remained very much a part of the Bears. The team owners, the McCaskey family, asked Payton to take a seat on the Bears' board of directors. Because of this, Payton was able to prove to the rest of the professional football community that he could do more than run a ball up and down the field. He wanted to show the NFL that he could manage a team, as well as play for it. The main reason Payton left the game was at the suggestion of his agent, Bud Holmes. Holmes thought the timing was perfect for Payton to take ownership of an NFL team. If he became an owner, he would be the first black man ever to do so. Having a black owner was important to other people in the NFL, especially Commissioner Pete Rozelle. The league wanted to open ownership to all races, not just whites. Payton needed an expansion team, a new football team created in a city that did not already have one, to become an owner. His chances were good until Rozelle retired in 1989. Paul Tagliabue was the new commissioner, and for him, Payton wasn't much more than another guy who wanted to own a football team.

Though he didn't have enough money to buy a major stake in a team, Payton wanted to play an active role as an owner and serve as a team president. Since the NFL was expanding at that time, the rare opportunity to be an owner seemed a reasonable possibility. Payton considered a few teams, such as the Oakland Raiders and the Carolina Panthers. But the most promising prospect was the St. Louis Cardinals. The big money man for St. Louis was James Orthwine, owner of beer-brewing company Anheuser-Busch. Jerry Clinton and Fran Murray (a part-owner of the New England Patriots) were also interested in the deal.

For almost four years, Payton promoted the city of St. Louis, trying to get the NFL to expand there. St. Louis got a team, the Cardinals, but Payton didn't get to be the owner. His partners, Murray, Clinton, and Orthwine, all argued over who would get to lead the team. The NFL noticed their disagreement and told the potential owners they had one month to figure things out. Orthwine formed an ownership team of wealthy investors; Payton was not invited to join them.

Though Payton did not expect the Cardinals deal to fall apart, he did do other business on the side during those four frustrating years of salesmanship and negotiations. This was smart, because Sweetness wasn't getting the same offers in 1991 that he had gotten immediately after retirement. Owning a business, whether it was an NFL team or a restaurant, was important to Payton. Edward Payton had taught his children to respect those who owned their own businesses. So as soon as he had money to invest, Payton became a partner in McFadden Ventures, a company that ran nightclubs. The company didn't make a lot of money, but Payton learned a lot from the experience.

One of his most famous business ventures—which still exists today in Aurora, Illinois—is Walter Payton's Roundhouse. The Roundhouse Complex includes a restaurant and brewery. It is also home to the Walter Payton Museum. Walter's beer, Payton Pilsner, was selected as the number one Bohemian Pilsner in the 2000 World Beer Cup competition. Payton frequently visited the restaurant, much to the delight of customers and

The Walter Payton Roundhouse is a popular destination for football fans. The illustration plans (*top left*), the interior pre-construction (*above logo*), the logo (*top right*), and the finished complex (*bottom*) are seen above.

employees. His Roundhouse partner, Mark Alberts, remembers that Payton would always enter the restaurant through the back door and talk to all the employees before heading out to the dining room or bar to greet patrons. At one Christmas party, Payton even put on an apron and served drinks to all of his employees. Things like that made him a beloved boss.

In early 1994, Payton lent his name to a venture called Walter Payton Power Equipment. The company rented and sold heavy equipment used on construction sites. Like with his other businesses, Payton took an active role when it came to dealing with people. His charisma and enthusiasm were great for business.

Payton loved cars and competition, so he found a business venture that combined the two: auto racing. Cars were serious business for Payton. He first began racing on a little-known circuit called Sports 2000. The cars were pretty simple—not nearly as fast as NASCAR but fast enough to race. After only a short time in the Sports 2000 circuit, Payton moved up to a class of race car called the GT-3.

Actor Paul Newman wanted Payton on his team, Newman Racing. Sweetness loved the GT-3 cars because they drove like regular cars but had no roof and could go up to 140 miles an hour. When he was out of the driver's seat, Payton was still very much a part of the action.

The Last Ride

Walter Payton stopped racing cars the day he got in an accident that could have killed him. The race was Road America in Elkhart Lake, Wisconsin. Payton's daughter, Brittney, who was seven years old at the time, was at the race with her dad. During the race, Payton's car flipped over two fences, spilled gasoline, caught on fire, and then landed upside down. Payton managed to pull himself out of the car and suffered only a burn on his neck, a few cuts, a mild concussion, and gasoline in his eye. Brittney was terrified that her father was badly hurt, and it took Payton a while to prove to her that he was OK. After that accident, Payton never raced again. His only involvement in the car racing circuit would be as an owner. Someone else could do the really dangerous stuff.

He would spend all the races in the pit, helping out and directing drivers.

Payton's generous and kind nature made his other post-football activities a perfect fit. In 1989, Payton and the family of George Halas, the Bears' first owner, founded the George Halas/Walter Payton Foundation. The foundation changed its name to reflect only Payton in 1998, and its mission is to provide "financial and motivational support to youth, and to help them realize that they can raise the quality of their lives, and the lives of those around them."

The foundation's biggest project every year is the Wishes for Santa program. Abused and neglected children in the Illinois Department of Children and Family Services get Christmas gifts and clothing, thanks to the generosity of Payton and others. In 1998, 35,000 children received gift bags of items worth about $100. The foundation also has a job placement program for teens and young adults, and sponsors many charity auctions of sports memorabilia.

Kim Tucker has been the executive director of the Walter Payton Foundation since 1993. In the early days, she said, the foundation mostly helped fund urban school programs. The first event she planned was on Thanksgiving Day in 1993. One of Walter's restaurants, Studebaker's, invited 650 underprivileged children for dinner and activities. It was at that dinner that the seeds for the Wishes for Santa program were planted, Tucker said. Santa Claus appeared at the dinner and caused one child to burst into tears. When Payton asked the little boy what was wrong, he said, "I can't believe it, I can't believe Santa Claus is here and that Santa would come all the way from the North Pole just to see me." Sweetness started to cry, too, and vowed he would somehow help make Christmas special for all children from troubled families.

Payton's desire to help people came from lessons he had learned from his father. The athlete said in *Never Die Easy*, "He told me when I was young that it was your responsibility, once you've had some success, to reach back and bring someone with you."

Sweetness Fading

In the summer of 1998, Walter Payton began to complain of stomach pain. He thought it was just the effects of some spoiled crab he had eaten in Panama on business, but the problem didn't go away. All of a sudden he was tired, a feeling he rarely experienced. He got pimples for the first time since he was a teenager, and the whites of his eyes grew yellow. In October, when he finally decided to go to the doctor, he wanted to go to the best. Payton chose the Mayo Clinic in Rochester, Minnesota, one of the most prestigious medical facilities in the country.

Payton couldn't get an appointment until early December, right about the time he started to lose weight. He lost 50 pounds in two months. At the Mayo Clinic, tests revealed that Payton had primary sclerosing cholangitis, or PSC. The disease, which is very rare, causes scarring and swelling of the bile ducts inside and outside the liver. Bile helps break down fat in the body, but when it cannot move in and out of the liver through the ducts, it can damage liver cells. There is no known cause for the disease, and the only chance for a cure is a liver transplant.

The doctors gave Sweetness a year or two to live without a new liver. His attitude about his illness was similar to the attitude that helped him win the Super Bowl, Payton told CNN's Larry King. "I realized that at this particular point the doctors that were working with me were the best in the business, so it was sort of like when I had Coach Ditka. I just said I'm going to believe in his philosophy and I'm going to do as he tells me because he's going to take us to the Super Bowl. It was the same way [here], I just used the same philosophy."

When Payton told his business partner, Mike Lanigan, about the illness, the former player's positive attitude shone through. Payton said he had good news and bad news.

Payton wept during a 1999 press conference in which he announced that he was suffering from a rare liver disease.

"Mikey, I'm not going to be around very much longer," Payton said. The good news? "I'm alive today." That was Payton's attitude throughout the rest of his illness, Lanigan said in *Never Die Easy*.

At first, Payton told only a few friends about his illness. He was a very private person, and he only wanted to fight the disease with the help of his family and doctors. Payton stayed out of the public eye until January 29, 1999, when his son Jarrett held a press conference to announce his decision to play football for the University of Miami. That night, a television reporter said on the local news that Payton looked sick. Sweetness decided he had to tell the public. With Connie and Jarrett at his side, Walter Payton had his own press conference and announced to the world that he was sick.

After the press conference, everyone wanted to talk to Payton. He appeared on *Larry King Live*, *The Oprah Winfrey Show*, and *CBS This Morning*. In one of these interviews, Payton said that this new challenge was no different than any other in his career. "It's just like football. You

Waiting for Life

People can sometimes wait years for organ transplants. All they can do is put their names on the United Network for Organ Sharing list and hope a healthy organ comes their way. People get organs in order of how sick they are, how long they've been waiting, their blood type, and other medical information. There are separate rules for each organ that determine which patients get a transplant. People on the transplant list don't get any special treatment. It doesn't matter if a patient is a president or a football star, they still have to wait their turn.

never know when or what your last play is going to be. You just play it because you love it. Same way with life. You live life because you love it. If you can't love it, you just give up hope."

Immediately after that, Payton sprang into action. All the effort he had previously put into football, he now put into his illness and the issue of organ donation. Payton made several appearances in support of organ donation and once appeared on television with a message about organ donation in conjunction with the television show *Touched by an Angel*. Because of Payton's electric personality, thousands of Americans signed up to be organ donors.

A few weeks after the press conference, Payton's doctors had more bad news. Not only did he have PSC, he also had cancer of the bile duct. Exploratory surgery revealed that the cancer had spread to Payton's lymph nodes. The diagnosis was grim: A transplant would do no good. Sweetness was going to die. Payton told few people about the new cancer diagnosis. Not even his children knew. Regardless, thousands of supportive letters poured into his office.

All the support and prayers of Payton's family and friends could not stop the inevitable. He was dying. He never complained, even while in wretched pain. Payton made the time he had left meaningful for himself and the ones he loved. His brother Eddie remembered that Payton was never bitter and never asked, "Why me?" He says in *Never Die Easy*, "For a man to go with that much pride and that much dignity just says volumes about who he was."

In late October 1999, Payton's kidneys failed. The only thing doctors could do was make him comfortable. Sweetness was his old self right to the end, six days later. Jarrett returned from college to be with the family. At one point when Jarrett left the house and returned, his father asked him, "Where have you been?" No matter where Jarrett was, his father always asked him that same question, whether he was coming from school or practice or spending time with friends. "I still smile when I think about it. That was actually the last thing that he said to me," Jarrett remembered in *Never Die Easy*.

Brittney Payton, who was very much her daddy's little girl, showed the same strength and poise as her father. Just 10 days before Payton died, Brittney accepted ESPN's ARETE Award for Courage. *Arete* is an ancient Greek word for "virtue," but a more exact definition is being the best one can be. Brittney, then only 14, spoke courageously on behalf of her ailing dad. "My father would like me to thank you for all the cards and prayers," she said, apologizing that her father could not be there himself.

From the earliest days of his illness, Payton's friend from the Bears, Matt Suhey, was there. Payton wouldn't let anyone except Suhey go to the doctor with him. In the final days before Payton died, Suhey was at the house every night. Before he would go, if Payton was asleep, he would wake him up to say good-bye, kiss him on the forehead, and tell him he loved him. Payton and Suhey watched tons of sporting events together. Suhey would take Payton out for drives, which he loved.

Just two weeks before he died, Payton played his last prank on Matt Suhey. They were out driving around and Payton said he wanted to visit former teammate Mike Singletary. Payton gave Suhey directions to the player's home. They got to the house and Suhey knocked on the door. Of course, it wasn't Mike Singletary's house at all. Suhey

Flags flew at half-staff at Chicago's Soldier Field on November 2, 1999, the day after Payton died of cancer.

was embarrassed, but Payton was sitting in the car laughing gleefully.

The support and love of family and friends could not stop the disease. Walter Payton died shortly after noon on November 1, 1999—All Saints' Day. Immediately, the family planned two memorial services, one private and one at Soldier Field for all Payton's fans. Just five hours after his father passed away, Jarrett offered a statement to the press. Among others, he thanked the Bears and their fans. "They said it was tough to understand the family relationship that exists

Payton's beloved family, daughter Brittney, son Jarrett, and wife Connie at a public tribute held for Sweetness at Chicago's Soldier Field

between teammates; I understand that more today. Finally, our greatest thanks goes out to the people of Chicago. You adopted my dad and made him yours. He loved you all. You have made this his home. We are proud to be among you."

Nearly 20,000 fans came to Soldier Field on November 6, 1999, to say good-bye to Walter Payton. Signs and number 34 jerseys dotted the crowd. Dozens of former and current Bears, as well as many NFL officials, were there to bid farewell to Sweetness. Commissioner Paul Tagliabue cited Payton's poise and style: "Walter

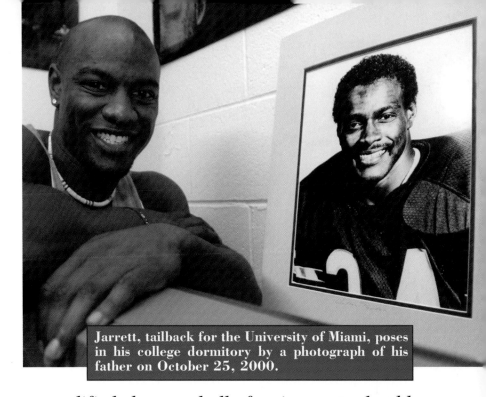

Jarrett, tailback for the University of Miami, poses in his college dormitory by a photograph of his father on October 25, 2000.

exemplified class, and all of us in sports should honor him by striving to perpetuate his standard of excellence. The tremendous grace and dignity he displayed in his final months reminded us again why 'Sweetness' was the perfect nickname for Walter Payton." Coach Mike Ditka, who spoke at Payton's private memorial service, said of his star player, "He was the best football player I've ever seen, and probably one of the best people I've ever met."

Timeline

July 25, 1954 Walter Jerry Payton born in Columbia, Mississippi.

1969 Starts playing football in eleventh grade at Columbia High School.

1974 Graduates in three and a half years with a bachelor of science in education from Jackson State University and as leading scorer in NCAA history. Scored 65 touchdowns and rushed for 3,563 yards.

January 28, 1975 The Chicago Bears make Payton their first pick in the NFL draft and fourth overall draft pick.

1976 Voted to first of nine Pro Bowls after his second season.

November 20, 1977 Rushes for NFL single-game record of 275 yards against Minnesota Vikings.

1977 At 23, is the youngest player to be voted NFL's Most Valuable Player after leading the league with 1,852 rushing yards.

1983 Opens Studebaker's, the first of several nightclubs he owned.

October 7, 1984 Breaks Jim Brown's career rushing record of 12,312 yards with 6-yard run against New Orleans.

January 26, 1986 The Bears beat the New England Patriots 46–10 to win Super Bowl XX, though Payton does not score.

1987 Signs a one-year, $1-million contract for final season with Bears.

December 20, 1987 Payton plays in final regular-season game and his number, 34, is retired. He leaves the NFL as the league's all-time leading rusher with 16,726 yards, a record that still stands.

January 10, 1988 Plays his final game, a play-off loss to the Washington Redskins.

1989 Establishes the Walter Payton Foundation to help abused and neglected children.

November 16, 1989 Becomes a partner in a group bidding to bring new NFL franchise to St. Louis, Missouri. Bid later fails in 1993.

January 30, 1993 Elected to Pro Football Hall of Fame.

March 21, 1996 Payton and three partners open Walter Payton's Roundhouse Complex, housing a brewery, a restaurant, and a museum, in Aurora, Illinois.

February 2, 1999 Payton announces that he has primary sclerosing cholangitis, a rare liver disease. His only chance is a transplant, but his hopes are dashed when a cancer diagnosis makes a transplant impossible.

April 12, 1999 Payton makes first public appearance since the announcement of his illness, throwing the first pitch at the Chicago Cubs' first home game.

November 1, 1999 Walter Payton dies at age forty-five.

Glossary

consistency Regularity; sameness.

cultivate To grow.

diligence Continuous effort or attention.

expansion team A new team that has been recently added to a sports league.

fervor Intensity of emotion.

fundamentals The basics of any sport or subject.

futile Useless; impossible.

gridiron Slang for football field.

hash mark Inbound lines on a football field that are 70 feet, 9 inches from each sideline.

Heisman Trophy An award given annually to the best college football player in the United States.

interracial Between two races, such as a friendship between a black person and white person.

lymph nodes Small bunches of tissue in the body
that produce lymphocytes, white blood cells,
that fight disease.

methodically Performed or arranged in an
orderly manner.

momentum Forward motion.

perfect season A season in which a team wins
every game it plays.

premier The best.

prestigious Well-respected.

primed Ready.

prowess Great ability or skill.

running back The player who starts at the back
of the field and, after getting the ball, runs
through defensive tacklers toward the end zone.

rush To run with the football.

segregate To separate people, usually by race.

unshakable Fearless; sturdy.

For More Information

The Chicago Bears
Halas Hall at Conway Park
1000 Football Drive
Lake Forest, IL 60045
Web site: http://www.chicagobears.com

The Pro Football Hall of Fame
2121 George Halas Drive NW
Canton, OH 44708
(330) 456-8207
Web site: http://www.profootballhof.com

The Walter and Connie Payton Foundation
104 North Barrington Road
Streamwood, IL 60107
(847) 605-0034
Web site: http://www.payton34.com

Walter Payton Cancer Fund
3150 Salt Creek Lane, Suite 118
Arlington Heights, IL 60005
(888) 221-2873
Web site:http://www.walterpaytoncancerfund.org

The Walter Payton Museum at Walter Payton's
 Roundhouse Complex
205 North Broadway
Aurora, IL 60505
(630) 264-BREW (2739)

Web Sites

Due to the changing nature of Internet links, the
Rosen Publishing Group, Inc., has developed an
online list of Web sites related to the subject of
this book. This site is updated regularly. Please
use this link to access the list:

http://www.rosenlinks.com/fhf/wap/

For Further Reading

H&S Media. *Sweetness: The Courage and Heart of Walter Payton*. Chicago: Triumph Books, 1999.

Italia, Bob. *Inside the NFL: The Chicago Bears*. Edina, MN: ABDO and Daughters, 1996.

Koslow, Philip. *Football Legends: Walter Payton*. Broomall, PA: Chelsea House Publishers, 1994.

Payton, Walter, and Don Yaeger. *Never Die Easy: The Autobiography of Walter Payton*. New York: Villard Books, 2000.

Towle, Mike. *I Remember Walter Payton: Personal Memories of Football's "Sweetest" Superstar and the People Who Knew Him Best*. Nashville, TN: Cumberland Books, 2000.

Bibliography

Associated Press. "'It's Really Sad to Me' Ditka Mourns Payton's Loss, Remembers His Life." CNNSI.com. November 1, 1999. Retrieved September 2001 (http://sportsillustrated.cnn.com/football/nfl/news/1999/11/01/payton_ditka_ap/index.html).

Associated Press: "'Sweetness' Remembered in Quotes." CNNSI.com. November 1, 1999. Retrieved September 2001 (http://sportsillustrated.cnn.com/football/nfl/news/1999/11/01/payton_quotes_ap).

Associated Press. "Walter Payton Dead at 45." CNNSI.com. November 2, 1999. Retrieved September 2001 (http://sportsillustrated.cnn.com/football/nfl/news/1999/11/01/payton_obit).

Attner, Paul. "Q&A: Hall of Fame Eve." SportingNews.com. August 2, 1993. Retrieved September 2001 (http://www.sportingnews.com/archives/payton/article1.html).

H&S Media. *Sweetness: The Courage and Heart of Walter Payton*. Chicago: Triumph Books, 1999.

Lamb, Kevin. "Payton, the Competitor." SportingNews.com. September 27, 1980. Retrieved September 2001 (http://www.sportingnews.com/archives/payton/article8.html).

Payton, Walter, and Don Yaeger. *Never Die Easy: The Autobiography of Walter Payton*. New York: Villard Books, 2000.

Telander, Rick: "Up and Over, To the Record and Beyond." CNNSI.com. October 15, 1984. Retrieved September 2001 (http://sportsillustrated.cnn.com/football/news/1999/10/29/payton_flashback_1984).

Index

A

Alberts, Mark, 84
Alcorn State (Mississippi), 25–27, 34
Anderson, Neal, 70–71
auto racing, 84–86

B

Boston, Charles, 21–22, 25, 27
Brown, Jim, 54, 56, 58–59, 62
Brown v. Board of Education, 17
Buffone, Doug, 42

C

CBS This Morning, 92
Chicago Bears, 5, 35–36, 38–39, 41–45, 48–50, 52, 54–55, 58–59, 62–65, 67–68, 70–72, 78, 80, 96, 98
Chicago, Illinois, 9, 36–37, 39–40, 45, 48, 50, 59, 68, 71, 98
Chicago Tribune, 13
Columbia, Mississippi, 12–13, 17, 19, 21–22, 41, 75

Columbia Wildcats, 19–21, 25, 27

D

Dallas Cowboys, 38, 48, 52
Ditka, Mike, 49, 52, 65, 68, 89, 99
Division I–AA, 11, 26
draft picks, 38–39

E

ESPN's ARETE Award for Courage, 95–96
expansion teams, 80

F

Finks, Jim, 72–73

H

Harper, Roland, 52–54
Harris, Franco, 56, 58
Heisman Trophy award, 38
Hill, Bob, 9, 30–33
Holmes, Bud, 78, 80

I

Illinois Department of Children and Family Services, 86

J

Jackson State Tigers, 30, 33–35
Jackson State University (Mississippi), 6, 19, 25–27, 30–32, 45, 72

K

King, Larry, 89

L

Landry, Tom, 38
Lanigan, Mike, 89, 92
Larry King Live, 92
LeGere, Bob, 64
linebackers, 33, 37, 65
Lott, Ronnie, 63

M

Mayo Clinic, 88–89
Minnesota Vikings, 49
MVP (Most Valuable Player) award, 48

N

NCAA (National Collegiate Athletic Association), 26
Never Die Easy, 16, 22, 25, 33, 40, 42, 54, 58, 65, 68, 71, 87, 92, 95
New England Patriots, 5, 67–68, 81
Newman, Paul, 85
Newman Racing team, 85
New Orleans Saints, 59

N

NFL (National Football League), 8–10, 25, 30–31, 34–35, 41–42, 45, 48–49, 62, 65, 67, 72, 75, 80–82, 98
Norwood, Connie, 6, 32–33, 45

O

Oprah Winfrey Show, The, 92
organ transplants, 10, 89, 93–94

P

Payton, Alyne, 12–14, 40
Payton, Brittney, 6, 85, 95–96
Payton, Eddie, 8, 13–15, 19, 27, 41–42, 94
Payton, Edward, 12, 14, 75, 82, 87
Payton, Jarrett, 6, 73, 92, 95, 97
Payton, Pam, 8, 13, 15
Payton, Walter
  awards and honors, 11, 35, 38, 48, 72–73, 75
  birth, 12
  childhood, 6, 8, 12–16
  death, 10, 36, 89, 92, 94, 97
  education, 6, 17, 19, 23, 35, 40
  illness and injuries, 9–10, 31, 43, 85, 88–89, 92–97
  marching band, 6, 17, 19
  marriage, 45

relationships with family, 6, 8–9, 13–14, 19, 27, 32–33, 40, 45, 50, 73, 75, 87, 92, 94–95, 97–98
relationship with the media, 8, 12, 27, 30, 34–35, 54, 62, 92
restaurant owner, 9, 82, 84
stats, 5, 9–10, 21, 35, 43, 45, 48, 56, 58, 62–63, 67, 71–72, 76–77
Payton Pilsner, 82
"Paytons' Place," 27
Penn State (Pennsylvania), 26, 53
Pittsburgh Steelers, 43, 56, 58
primary sclerosing cholangitis (PSC), 9–10, 89, 94
Pro Bowl games, 72
Pro Football Hall of Fame, 6, 9, 11, 14, 71–73, 75
Pro Football Weekly, 64

R
racial discrimination, 6, 17, 19–21, 23, 26, 35
running backs, 5, 8, 19, 33, 37, 43, 48, 78

S
San Francisco 49ers, 48, 63–64
Seattle Seahawks, 56, 58
Singletary, Mike, 65, 96
Soul Train, 32

Southeastern Conference (SEC), 23, 25, 27
Southwestern Athletic Conference (SWAC), 27, 34
Sporting News, The, 56
St. Louis Cardinals, 81–82
Studebaker's, 87
Suhey, Matt, 52–53, 96
Super Bowl games, 5–6, 49–50, 52, 55, 58, 62, 64, 67–68, 70, 89
"Super Bowl Shuffle, The," 67
Super Bowl XX, 5–6, 55, 67–68, 70

T
Tagliabue, Paul, 80, 98
Touched by an Angel, 94
Tucker, Kim, 86–87

U
United Network for Organ Sharing, 93

W
Walter Payton Award, 11
Walter Payton Foundation, 86–87
Walter Payton Museum, 82
Walter Payton's Roundhouse Complex, 82, 84
Washington Redskins, 63, 70
Wishes for Santa, 86–87

About the Author

Aileen Gallagher is a freelance reporter and editor. She has written for various legal, financial, and general-interest publications, in print and online. Her work has appeared in the *New York Law Journal*, TheStreet.com, the *National Law Journal*, and Law.com. She lives and writes in New York City.

Photo Credits

Cover, pp. 10, 18, 26, 41, 69, 72, 74, 79, 90–91, 97, 99 © AP/Wide World Photos; pp. 4, 24, 28–29, 34, 39, 44, 46–47, 53, 57, 60–61, 77 © Bettmann/ Corbis; p. 7 © Heinz Kleutmeier/Timepix; p. 15 © Bruce Burkhardt/Corbis; p. 37 © Bill Ross/Corbis; p. 51 © Icon SMI; pp. 66, 83 courtesy of the Walter Payton Museum; p. 98 © Reuters New Media, Inc./Corbis.

Series Design and Layout

Tahara Hasan